Improving
STRENGTH
AND POWER

Paul Mason

WAYLAND

First published in 2016 by Wayland
Copyright © Wayland 2016

Wayland, an imprint of Hachette Children's Group
Part of Hodder & Stoughton
Carmelite House
50 Victoria Embankment
London EC4Y 0DZ

Editor: Julia Adams
Designer: Tim Mayer, Mayer Media
Proofreader and indexer: Claire Shanahan
Picture researcher: Kathy Lockley
Consultant: Professor John Brewer

British Library Cataloguing in Publication Data
Mason, Paul, 1967-
  Training for sport.
  Improving strength.
  1. Muscle strength--Juvenile literature. 2. Physical
  fitness--Nutritional aspects--Juvenile literature.
  I. Title
  613.7'1-dc22

ISBN: 9780750297646
Library ebook ISBN: 9780750276795
10 9 8 7 6 5 4 3 2 1

Printed in China

An Hachette UK company
www.hachette.co.uk
www.hachettechildrens.co.uk

Websites
The website addresses (URLs) included in this book were
valid at the time of going to press. However, because of the
nature of the Internet, it is possible that some addresses may
have changed, or sites may have changed or closed down
since publication. While the author and publisher regret any
inconvenience this may cause the readers, no responsibility
for any such changes can be accepted by either the author
or the publisher.

Disclaimer
During the preparation of this book, all due care has been
taken with regard to the advice, activities and techniques
described and depicted. The publishers regret that they can
accept no liability for any loss or injury sustained.

Picture acknowledgements:
Al Bello/Getty Images: 9
Robert Cianflone/Getty Images: 14
Michael Cole/Corbis: 28TR
Andy Crawford: 15TR
Mark Dadswell/Staff/Getty Images: 29
empipe/Shutterstock: 26 (top)
FRANCK FIFE/AFP/Getty Images: Title page, 8
Chris Floyd/Reportage/Getty Images: 20
foodfolio/Alamy: 28BL
Bill Greenblatt/Liaison/Getty Images: 25
Paul Hanna/Reuters/Corbis: 22-23B
Frederic Haslin/TempSport/Corbis: 23CL
huaxiadragon/iStock: background images throughout
AdrianHillman/iStock images: folios throughout
Alexander Ishchenko/Shutterstock: COVER (small, top)
JeP /Shutterstock: COVER (small, bottom)
Herbert Kratky/Shutterstock: COVER (small, middle)
Robert Kwiatek/Rex Features: 13
Barry Lewis/Corbis: 19
Tom Lynn/Sports Illustrated/Getty Images: COVER, 5
Chris McGrath/Getty Images: 24
Robert Michael/Corbis: 6
MistikaS/iStock: background images throughout
KAZUHIRO NOGI/AFP/Getty Images: 4
ogergo/iStock: background images throughout
ED OUDENAARDEN/AFP/Getty Images: 15
prism68/Shutterstock: 26 (bottom)
Quinn Rooney/Getty Images: 7, 21
EVARISTO SA/AFP/Getty Images: 17
Filip Singer/isifa/Getty Images: 27B
Keren Su/China Span/Getty Images: 22CR
Topham Picturepoint/TopFoto.co.uk: 11
AHMAD YUSNI/AFP/Getty Images: 12

Contents

What is strength?

Strength is the ability to push against resistance. Try and push a car up a hill, and you meet resistance. To overcome it, you need to be very strong indeed. Weightlifters are strong – they can pick up over 400 kilograms. That's the equivalent of two men sitting on each end of the bar (four men in total)!

Strongman competitors, as you might guess, need tremendous maximum strength. They use it for picking up giant stones, pulling trucks and throwing weights high into the air. But where does their strength come from? It comes from their muscles.

China's Linlin Deng competes at the 2008 Beijing Olympics. Gymnasts need to be strong, but in a different way from a weightlifter.

Strength and muscles

Muscles are the parts of your body that move your joints, the places where bones meet. Wrap your left hand around your upper right arm, then lift your right fist towards your shoulder. You will feel the muscle on top of your arm (called your biceps) contracting as it pulls the joint closed. Then, as you lower your arm, your biceps relaxes and your triceps (the muscle on the bottom) contracts.

Your strength is mainly decided by the size and number of the fibres that make up your muscles. It is also linked to the type of fibres the muscles contain. Muscles contain fast-twitch and slow-twitch fibres. Fast-twitch ones are used when more than 25 per cent of your maximum strength is needed. Some people have more fast-twitch fibres than others, and these people are best suited to sports involving speed, strength and power.

Body types

Your body type also affects how much strength you can develop. Some people are born with genes that mean they naturally grow up to be broad and thick-bodied, with large muscles all over their body. But if that isn't you, don't despair! It's possible for everyone to improve their strength, given the right knowledge and training.

Naim Suleymanoglu, on his way to winning a third Olympic weightlifting gold, at the Atlanta Games in 1996.

Naim Suleymanoglu

Sport: Weightlifting

Country: Turkey

Born: 23 January 1967

Proof that you don't have to be big to be strong, Suleymanoglu was known as The Pocket Hercules during his weightlifting career. Suleymanoglu was born in Bulgaria, but from a Turkish family. He first became famous when he set a world weightlifting record when he was just 16 years old.

After being forced by Bulgaria's rulers to change his name to the more Bulgarian-sounding Shalamanov, Suleymanoglu left the country in 1986. He became a Turkish citizen, and Turkey paid Bulgaria US$1,000,000 so that Suleymanoglu could compete for Turkey at the Olympics. He soon repaid the debt:

- In 1988, 1992 and 1996, Suleymanoglu won gold medals in the featherweight weightlifting division.
- He also won the World Championships seven times, the European Championships six times, and set 46 world records.

Suleymanoglu retired in 2000, after failing to win a fourth Olympic gold at the Sydney Games.

5

Strength in sport

Strength is important in a wide variety of sports. But athletes need to develop different kinds of strength, depending on the sport they take part in. Footballers, strongmen and cricketers all need to be strong in different ways, for example. So, what are the different kinds of strength, and what types of sport are they most useful for?

Maximum strength

Maximum strength is what most people probably think of when they hear the word 'strength'. It describes the maximum amount of force an athlete can generate in one muscle contraction.

Maximum strength is most important in events such as weightlifting and strongman contests. In these, the athletes must pick up or move heavy weights in a single movement. All their muscles together must generate the biggest possible force.

Power

Power is the ability to generate force quickly, with a fast muscle contraction. Power is important in speed-based events, such as:

- Sprinting (on foot, on a bike or in the water)
- Gymnastics, ice skating and other sports that need explosive power as part of their routine.
- Combat sports, such as boxing, judo and taekwondo.

Strength endurance

Strength endurance is the ability to develop force repeatedly. Football midfielders, bowlers in cricket, or tennis players, for example, have to perform the same action again and again. To keep doing so with the same force, they need good strength endurance.

Sprinters need explosive strength to fire themselves out of the starting blocks.

Weight training

One of the most common ways of developing strength is through weight training. It is important that weight training is adapted to the type of strength you want to develop, because each type of strength develops in a slightly different way. Developing tremendous maximum strength is less important for a footballer, for example, than working on power.

Rebecca Romero on track for another Olympic medal, at the Beijing Olympics in 2008.

PROFESSIONAL PROFILE

Rebecca Romero

Sport: Rowing, cycling

Country: UK

Born: 24 January 1980

Romero is a very unusual athlete, having reached the top level at not one but two extremely demanding sports: rowing and cycling. Both sports demand a tricky combination of power and endurance.

Romero's first sport was rowing, in which she won a silver medal at the 2004 Athens Olympics. She retired from rowing with a back injury in 2006.

Like rowing, cycling requires powerful leg and shoulder muscles. Romero found it relatively easy to adapt, and she was good enough to win World Championship gold in both individual and team pursuit.

Romero went to the 2008 Olympic Games as one of the red-hot favourites. She was also the first-ever British woman to compete in two different sports at summer Olympics. When she won gold in the individual pursuit, Romero became only the second woman in history to get medals for two different summer Olympic sports.

Body shapes

All of us are born with slightly different genes. Genes make up the code inside your body that decides things such as the colour of your eyes and hair. Genes also decide what shape your body will be – and this can have a big effect on the kind of sport you are likely to be good at. Scientists divide body shapes into three extremes: endomorph, ectomorph and mesomorph.

Endomorphs

An extreme endomorph has a pear-shaped body, with wide hips and shoulders, and is thicker front-to-back than side-to-side. They carry a lot of body fat on their upper legs, body and upper arms.

Endomorphs are typically able to develop tremendous strength. They are ideally suited to strength sports such as weightlifting, strongman, and hammer and discus throwing. Because of their weight, endomorphs tend to be less good at running sports, but their large lungs may help them to become good at sports such as rowing.

Ectomorphs

Ectomorphs are almost the opposite shape to endomorphs. They have narrow shoulders, chest and hips, long, slim arms and legs, and have very little fat on their body.

Ectomorphs are best suited to endurance sports such as distance running, where their low

Australian hooker Stephen Moore uses his strength to power through a tackle in a 2009 match against France. Rugby has positions for athletes of all shapes and sizes, from endomorphic props and hookers to ectomorphic lock forwards.

weight is an advantage. They find it difficult to build muscle mass, so strength sports present severe challenges to ectomorphs.

Mesomorphs

Mesomorphs have a triangular body, with wide shoulders and narrow hips. They carry little body fat, and are well muscled on their arms, legs and body. Mesomorphs adapt well to training, so they are able to include more strength, power or endurance work, depending on what sport they are taking part in.

Almost there! Matthias Steiner, split seconds away from Olympic glory in 2008.

Matthias Steiner

Sport: Weightlifting

Country: Austria, Germany

Born: 25 August 1982

Matthias Steiner's story is a rollercoaster ride of great achievements and great sadness. He has overcome terrible setbacks to become Olympic champion in weightlifting.

Steiner was born in Austria, and spent his career up until 2005 competing as an Austrian. Despite being diagnosed with diabetes at the age of 18, he was determined to train as a weightlifter.

In 2005, Steiner fell out with the Austrian weightlifting federation. At the same time he met and fell in love with a German woman, Susann. He moved to Germany and applied for German citizenship. This meant it would be three years before he could enter international competitions again.

In 2007, Susann was tragically killed in a car accident. The next year, at the Beijing Olympics, Steiner was determined to put in a performance that would honour his wife's memory. Despite going into the final round of lifts behind, he put in a monumental effort to clean and jerk 258 kg. It was enough to overtake the remaining competitors. As he was awarded his gold medal, Steiner clutched a photo of his wife.

Somatotyping

Somatotyping is a way of describing your body type using numbers. It is useful because none of us is a pure endomorph, mesomorph or ectomorph. We all have a bit of each type. Because each body type is better suited to particular sports, knowing your somatotype score can be useful in deciding what kind of sport you are most likely to be good at.

Somatotype scoring

Somatotyping gives you a score according to how strongly you have the characteristics of each body type. With hardly any of the characteristics, you score a 1. With all of the characteristics, you score a 7, the maximum. The scores are given in the order endomorph, mesomorph, ectomorph. A pure endomorph would have a score of 711, a mesomorph would score 171, and an ectomorph 117.

Somatotype diagrams

A somatotype diagram looks a bit like a pyramid, with mesomorphic bodies at the tip. As the body shape trickles down the left or right, the type of sport that the subject is likely to be best at changes. Along the left side are the maximum-strength athletes: wrestlers, strongmen, and weightlifters. On the right are those who would be best at endurance sports.

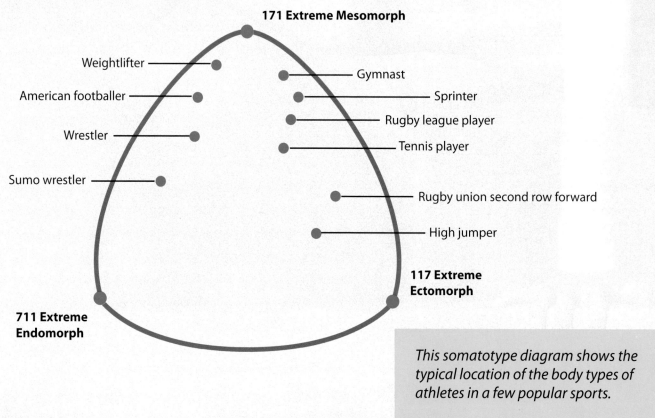

This somatotype diagram shows the typical location of the body types of athletes in a few popular sports.

Konishiki

Sport: Sumo wrestling

Country: Hawaii, USA; Japan

Born: 31 December 1963

Konishiki is a Hawaiian-born expert in the Japanese martial art of sumo wrestling. He was the first foreign-born sumo ever to reach the rank of *ozeki*, the second-highest grade. Konishki – whose nickname was The Dump Truck – was also the heaviest sumo ever.

Konishiki originally wanted to become a lawyer, but went to Japan to train as a sumo at the age of 18. He rose quickly to the rank of *ozeki* before knee injuries – made worse as his weight increased to over 250 kg – caused his career to stall.

Konishiki made a brilliant comeback from injury, and by March 1992 he had a recent tournament record of 38 wins and 7 losses. He had also won three major championships. Promotion to *yokozuna*, sumo's highest rank, seemed certain. But in his next tournament, The Dump Truck won only 9 of his 15 bouts, and promotion never came.

Konishiki retired in 1997, and is still a popular celebrity in Japan. He has appeared in several TV shows and movies, and worked as a radio DJ. Konishiki is also a keen musician, mixing rap and ukulele playing in an unlikely combination.

Konishki faces up to a small-but-determined opponent, who doesn't seem to be making much progress.

11

Strength and weight

All athletes have to balance the need for strength against weight and endurance. Strength comes from big, heavy muscles, which use up energy like a space rocket heading for orbit. Smaller muscles are more like a moped. It may not be as powerful as a space rocket – but it would get you a lot further on the same amount of fuel.

Adapting weight training

Many athletes use weight training to improve the way their muscles work. How they do this must be adapted to the kind of sport they do:

- Pure strength events require big, powerful muscles that can generate high maximum power. These are built up using heavy weights, with each exercise done just a few times.

- If speed-endurance is an important part of your sport, slightly lighter weights are most useful. The exercises will be repeated more times: this helps build up the muscle's ability to keep working for longer.

- For endurance athletes, strength and power are less important than the ability to keep working for a long time. They use lighter weights, with the exercises done a greater number of times.

Mariusz Pudianowski competes in a strongman competition is Kuala Lumpur, Malaysia. This particular event is known as the 'Farmer's Walk'.

Body mass

Muscle fibres are dense and relatively heavy, so increasing the size of your muscles increases your body mass. After a long period of strength training, the scales may read higher – 68 kg instead of 65 kg, for example – even though you are in better shape. This may seem a bit surprising, but it is nothing to worry about unless the increase is large.

The increase in body mass caused by strength training has an important side effect. Many health professionals assess body weight using charts that allow them to look along a line according to a patient's height, and discover whether they are underweight, the correct weight or overweight. Strength athletes often come out as overweight on these charts – even though they are fit and healthy.

Don't try this at home: Pudzianowski takes a 41-tonne airplane for a walk.

Mariusz
Pudzianowski

Sport: Strongman

Country: Poland

Born: 7 February 1977

Pudzianowski is one of the world's greatest strongman competitors. He has won the World's Strongest Man title five times – more than anyone else – and goes by the nickname Super Mariusz.

Strongman contests make very specific demands of the competitors. Some come from weightlifting backgrounds, but most specialise in strongman competitions. Events include pulling trucks along on a rope, picking up cars, carrying giant rocks, and throwing heavy weights over high bars.

Pudzianowski won the World's Strongest Man in 2002 and 2003. The second year, he won by the biggest-ever amount. In 2004 Pudzianowski placed third, but was later disqualified for using illegal drugs. Over the years, many people in power-based events have been caught using illegal drugs, particularly anabolic steroids and stimulants, to improve their performance. He was banned from competing for one year.

Pudzianowski returned from his ban as formidable as ever. He won World's Strongest Man again in 2005, 2007 and 2008.

Core stability

Core stability describes the strength of the muscles that support your body's trunk or torso. It is also sometimes called core strength. The most important core muscles are the ones that support the spine. Core stability is important to all sportspeople, because it affects both strength and technique.

Core stability and strength

Core stability is particularly important for people taking part in strength-based sports. For example, imagine a weightlifter doing the clean and jerk. They need powerful arm, shoulder and leg muscles that work together to pick up a heavy weight. But if the lifter's core muscles are weak, then the connection between upper and lower body will buckle under the strain. However strong their arms and legs, the lifter's core will be a weak link in the chain, and will limit their performance.

Core stability and technique

Good core stability is needed in all sports, because it has an effect on how efficiently an athlete can put their technique into action. As an example, imagine a kayaker in a slalom race. They have to paddle strongly for speed, but also to keep the boat as steady and smooth in the water as possible. Without strong muscles in their torso, this would be impossible.

Jenna Myers of Australia showing good weightlifting technique. Her back is straight and her arms fully extended, so that her legs can power the lift.

In many sports – for example, discus throwing, judo or gymnastics – using core muscles as part of your technique adds extra strength and power.

Core stability and injury

Good core stability helps prevent injuries, by making it less likely that the body will be twisted in a dangerous way. In particular, it helps prevent injury to the spine or spinal muscles.

The twists and turns of judo competition demand excellent core strength, whether you are defending or attacking.

Test your core stability

Put a watch on the ground where you can see it. Assume a press-up-like position, forearms flat on the ground and on your toes. It is important to keep your back straight throughout these exercises. Apart from the first and last exercises, try to hold each position for 15 seconds:

- Hold the basic position for 60 seconds
- Now lift your right arm off the ground and hold the position
- Return to the basic position, then lift your left arm off the ground
- From the basic position, next lift your right leg off the ground
- Return to the basic position, then lift your left leg off the ground
- Next lift your left leg and right arm off the ground
- Return to the basic position, then lift your right leg and left arm off the ground
- Go back to the basic press-up position and hold it for 30 seconds

If you can do this, you have good core strength. If not, repeating the routine 3 or 4 times a week will help you to improve. Measure progress in how close to the 15-second timings for each position you can get, or how far through the routine you can get.

Increasing strength

Muscles improve their performance when they are forced to work harder than normal. To improve a muscle's strength, most athletes use weight training, resistance training or a combination of the two.

Resistance training

Resistance training is when the muscle or muscles are trying to overcome an opposing force greater than the one they would usually meet. One of the simplest examples is trying to run through water, which offers more resistance than air. Another is the swim-bench, on which swimmers lie to practise their strokes, by pulling on paddles attached to pulleys. The pulley can be set to feel like the resistance swimmers feel in water, or it can be set to offer greater resistance. Other resistance-training devices include exercise bikes and rowing machines.

Weight training

The most popular way to increase muscle size is through weight training. It is possible to target very specific muscles and groups of muscles using weight training. Athletes rely on their coaches to help them do this, but there is also advice on sources of weight-training workouts for specific sports on page 31 if this book.

Tennis players develop very specific strength in their racquet arm and shoulder, allowing them to add power to their strokes.

Physical effects of strength training

Strength training has three key effects on the body:

1) Muscle hypertrophy – an increase in the size of the individual fibres that make up a muscle

2) An increase in the size and density of bones (which steadily become stronger to bear the extra load)

3) An increase in the amount of energy stored in the muscles, which the body calls on during the first 60–120 seconds of hard activity.

When muscles increase in size, they sometimes become less able to make a wide range of movement. This makes it important to combine flexibility work with strength training.

Stepanka Hilgertova

Sport: Kayak slalom

Country: Czechoslovakia, Czech Republic

Born: 10 April 1968

Stepanka Hilgertova is one of the most successful kayak slalom racers ever. She was at the top of this demanding sport for 16 years, taking part in an amazing six Olympic Games.

Kayak slalom requires great power, as the racers are often forced to turn their boats and paddle upstream, into the teeth of a raging current. They must get the boat going fast enough to carry on through a gate, before swinging round on the current and continuing downstream. To have raced kayak slalom at six Olympics, winning two gold medals, is an amazing achievement.

Hilgertova's Olympic career began in 1992, when she came 12th. At the 1996 Olympics, at the age of 28, she struck gold. This was followed by a second gold in 2000, at the age of 32. Many people would then have retired, but not Hilgertova. She went on to place 5th in the 2004 Athens Games, and 9th in the 2008 Beijing Games. By then, Hilgertova was 40 years old, and eligible to take part in masters competitions!

Stepanka Hilgertova powers through the gates at the World Slalom Championships in 2007.

Training for maximum strength

Maximum strength is usually increased through weight training. Athletes lift close to their maximum possible weight. They perform a small number of repetitions – sometimes as few as one, and rarely more than five – before they have to rest.

Weight training rules

Weight training carries a risk of injury. This is especially true when training to increase maximum strength, because the muscles are working at or near their maximum possible range. It is also possible to damage muscles, tendons and ligaments by doing exercises incorrectly, or simply through an accident in the gym. Following a few basic rules can make weight training much safer:

- Always warm up before weight training. The aim of the warm-up is to increase your body temperature, and to prepare the muscles you are going to be exercising.

- Never train alone: if there's an injury or accident, there won't be anyone there to help.

- Don't over-train (see pages 24 and 25 for more information about this). Allow your body plenty of time to recover from hard training sessions.

1-repetition maximum (1RM)

Weighttraining guides sometimes talk about 1RM, short for 1-reptition maximum. This is the maximum amount of weight an athlete should lift for a particular exercise. It is calculated using a complicated mathematical formula, and is best worked out by a coach.

1RM is a measure of an athlete's strength. If your 1RM figure increases for a particular exercise, it means the muscles used in that exercise are getting stronger.

Repetitions

The number of times you repeat a weight-training exercise is called repetitions. How many repetitions athletes do is governed by what percentage of their 1RM figure they are working at. Training above 80 per cent of 1RM leads to an increase in strength. This table gives a guide to how many repetitions should be done at given percentages:

Per cent of 1RM	Repetitions
60	17
65	14
70	12
75	10
80	8
85	6
90	5
95	3
100	1

Electrical muscle training

Muscle movement is stimulated by a tiny electrical charge from the central nervous system. Research has shown that whichever weight-training activity requires the biggest electrical charge from the central nervous system will produce the biggest gains in muscle growth.

The labels to the diagram show some key muscles, plus the most effective exercise for improving strength in them.

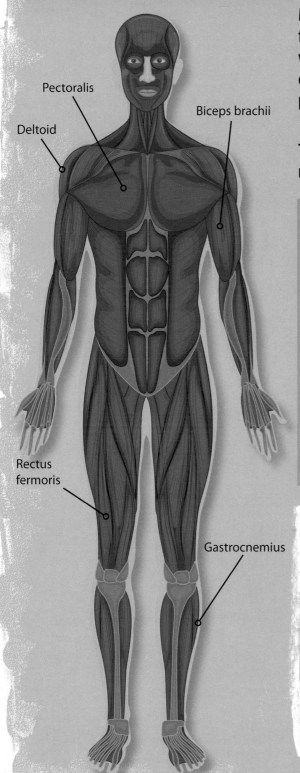

Pectoralis

Deltoid

Biceps brachii

Rectus fermoris

Gastrocnemius

Muscle:	Exercise:
Pectoralis	Dumbbell bench press
Deltoids	Standing dumbbell laterals
Biceps brachii	Incline seated dumbbell curls (alternate)
Triceps	Triceps press down (angled bar)
Latissimus dorsi	One arm dumbbell rows (alternate)
Rectus femoris	Seated leg extensions
Biceps femoris	Standing leg curls
Semitendinosus	Seated leg curls
Gastrocnemius	Standing one leg calf raises

Women generally have less muscle than men, because they have less testosterone, a chemical that helps the body to increase muscle mass. But there are exceptions, such as this competitor at the 1996 British Bodybuilding Championships.

Training for power

In many sports, strength alone is not enough. The strength also needs to be delivered as fast as possible. This kind of strength that allows you to push against something in a fast, strong movement is usually called power. Sprinters, gymnasts, people taking part in combat sports, ice skaters and many other athletes all find that improving their power improves their overall performance.

Targeting fast-twitch muscles

Power training (like all strength training) targets fast-twitch muscle fibres. Most people have roughly 50 per cent fast-twitch and 50 per cent slow-twitch muscle fibres, but some of us have a higher proportion of fast-twitch ones. Those are the people who make it to Olympic finals for the 100 metres, become famous point guards, or make it in the Premier League.

Improving power

Power can be improved in a variety of ways. Weight training improves the athlete's basic strength (see pages 16–19). To add speed, athletes may use some or all of the following:
- plyometrics: the use of jumping, leaping and bounding exercises. These train muscles to produce their strength more quickly.

- complex training: a session of resistance training, followed by plyometric exercises aimed at the same muscles

Former world 100-metres record holder Asafa Powell of Jamaica (in the grey/yellow T-shirt) takes part in plyometric training.

- medicine-ball training: quickly catching and returning a heavy medicine ball, as a way of increasing the speed at which a muscle can work

- conditioning exercises, which help to keep the athlete's entire body working well. These would include core-stability training, and exercises targeted at the athlete's particular sport. A sprinter, for example, might do rat-a-tats: running on the spot on their toes for bursts of 20–30 seconds, lifting their feet just a few centimetres off the ground.

Chris Hoy in full flight, powering round the final bend of a track race.

Chris Hoy

Sport: Track cycling

Country: UK

Born: 23 March 1976

Chris Hoy is, simply, one of the most powerful track cyclists ever. His heavily muscled body and incredible acceleration made him the racer all other riders fear. He is the most successful male Olympic cyclist in history.

As a youngster, Hoy raced BMX (some stories say he was inspired to take it up after seeing the movie *E.T.*). He also rowed for the Scotland junior team. But in 1994 he began concentrating on track cycling. He started to specialise in the 1-km time trial (which is known as the kilo) and the team pursuit.

In 2002, Hoy won team pursuit and kilo gold medals at the world championships. He quickly became the world's best kilo rider. This event demands raw power: Hoy won world titles again in 2004, 2006 and 2007. He also won the Olympic title in 2004.

Hoy's greatest year yet came in 2008. At the Beijing Olympics he won three golds: keirin, team sprint, and individual sprint. He won a further two gold medals at the London 2012 Olympics.

Training for strength endurance

Strength endurance describes an athlete's ability to continue to put out high levels of power over time. For example, imagine two sprinters who can both run 60 metres in seven seconds. But one runs 100 metres in 11.5 seconds, the other runs in 12 seconds. The first runner has better strength endurance. They are able to lay down the power for longer.

Energy for strength

When our muscles have to produce a lot of power quickly, they produce their energy without using oxygen from the bloodstream. This is known as anaerobic energy production. Most people's muscles contain only enough energy stores for between one and two minutes of anaerobic energy production.

A key aim of strength endurance training is to improve the time for which the muscles can work anaerobically. The muscles need to get better at storing and using energy. This happens when the muscles are repeatedly taken into anaerobic energy production.

Lactic acid and fatigue

One by-product of anaerobic energy production is lactic acid. The longer anaerobic exercise goes on, the more lactic acid is produced. Lactic acid causes fatigue – tiredness that makes exercise uncomfortable or painful. In the end, there is so much acid that the muscles cannot work properly.

Improving strength endurance

Weight and resistance training are the most common ways of improving the strength element of strength endurance. One of the most popular ways of improving the endurance element is circuit training.

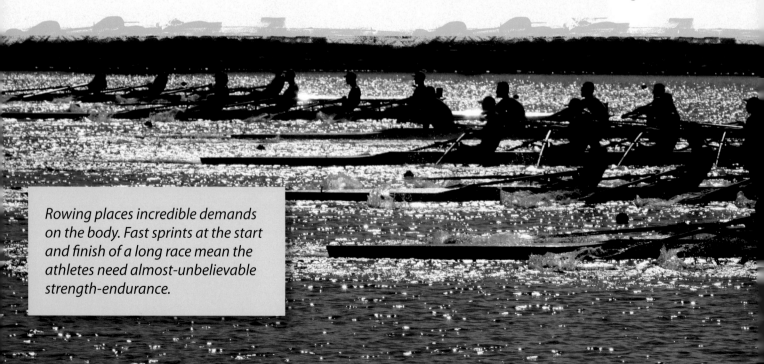

Rowing places incredible demands on the body. Fast sprints at the start and finish of a long race mean the athletes need almost-unbelievable strength-endurance.

In circuit training, between six and 10 strength exercises are done in different zones. The exercises might include press-ups, sit-ups, step-ups and skipping. The athletes do each exercise for a set period of time, then have a brief rest before moving on to the next exercise. Once the circuit of exercises is completed, the athletes have a longer rest before doing another circuit.

A young Steve Redgrave at the 1995 World Rowing Championships, where he won one of his nine World-Championship gold medals.

Steve Redgrave

Sport: Rowing

Country: UK

Born: 10 April 1968

Steve Redgrave is one of the world's most remarkable sportsmen, and the best Olympic rower in history. His biggest achievements are unlikely to ever be equalled:

- Gold medals at 5 consecutive Olympic Games, from 1984 to 2000. Only four athletes have ever managed this feat.
- Nine rowing World Championships gold medals.

Rowers tend to be large and powerful, but even among rowers Redgrave is a big man. He is 1.95 metres tall, and his competition weight was about 100 kg.

Oarsmen usually specialise in rowing either a left or right-side oar. They develop muscles that to allow them to apply maximum power to that specific side of the boat. Redgrave's tremendous natural strength allowed him to row both sides of the boat. He is one of very few rowers to have won Olympic gold medals from both left and right oars.

For most of his career, Redgrave battled against a serious digestive illness. From 1997, he also suffered from diabetes, making his nutrition requirements even more complicated.

Overtraining

In any area of sport, one of the biggest dangers is overtraining. The risks of overtraining are particularly serious in strength training, where muscles and joints are regularly pushed as hard as possible.

Signs of overtraining

Overtraining shows its effects in three key areas, which provide warning signs that an athlete's programme is too demanding:

1) Technique: old technique problems reappear, you find it harder to correct problems, and keeping a rhythm becomes increasingly difficult.

2) Physical condition: tiredness, lack of endurance, physical inability to change or follow tactics during competition.

3) Mental ability: reduced appetite for competition and training, irritability, and inability to accept or act on criticism.

Causes of overtraining

Problems caused by overtraining can result from one or more of the following:

- Not allowing proper recovery times. After a hard training session or competition, your body needs at least 24 hours to recover. Doing more hard training too soon means your body is still tired, so it will be impossible to get near to your highest levels of performance.

- Failing to use light sessions as a vehicle for recovery. All coaches include lighter training sessions in their schedules. These aid recovery, but the athlete must not work harder than planned.

- Making training more demanding too quickly. There are no short cuts in sports training: making training a lot harder each week will just make you more tired, because you are working closer to your maximum.

Kamran Panjavi of Great Britain injures his back at the 2004 Olympic Games in Athens. Injuries can be caused or made worse by overtraining.

It might give you the illusion that you're getting faster, but you won't be.

- Over-competing is a form of overtraining, as it means your body is doing too much work at maximum effort.

- Relying too heavily on a single training method may increase the risk of injury. It makes the muscles that are used more fatigued than a varied training schedule.

- Poor nutrition: not providing your body with the right foods.

- Too much complicated technique work done when tired or without adequate recovery can easily lead to injury.

On your marks... Get set... Magnus ver Magnusson about to start towing a large, heavy truck during a strongman contest.

Magnus ver Magnusson

Sport: Strongman
Country: Iceland
Born: 23 April 1963

Magnus ver Magnusson is a former strongman and powerlifter. He won World's Strongest Man contest four times between 1991 and 1996. Magnusson once held the world record for deadlifting a tyre, at 445 kg. That's the same weight as a couple of large mountain gorillas.

Magnusson first took part in a strongman event in 1985, when he finished third in Iceland's Strongest Man. The winner was another great Icelandic strongman (who also won the World's Strongest Man contest four times), Jon Pall Sigmarsson.

Magnusson continued to improve his contest results, and in 1991 he won the World's Strongest title for the first time. Amazingly, it was only after this that he decided to concentrate on strongman contests full-time. He came second in 1992 and 1993, and won the title again in 1994, 1995 and 1996.

Biomechanics and levers

Biomechanics is the application of mechanical principles to the human body. These principles help us to understand how our bones, joints and muscles work together to provide movement. Knowing this, it is possible for coaches to adjust their athletes' technique so that they get the most from their strength and power.

Biomechanics at work

Some sportspeople at first question how biomechanics can help them to improve their performance. One example of how it helps comes from cycling. Professional cyclists know that the height at which they set their saddle will have a significant effect on their pedalling power:

- If the saddle is too low, the rider will not be able to apply their muscles through a full range of movement. It will also be impossible to use the strong muscles of the cyclist's lower back.

- With the saddle set too high, the cyclist cannot apply full power right through the pedalling action, as their legs will not properly reach the pedals all the time.

- If the saddle is at the right height, power can be applied right through the pedal stroke. The strong muscles of the back and hips can be used as to help power the pedalling movement.

This rider has his saddle too high, as you can see from the way his left foot is forced to stretch down at an angle. As a result, the bottom of his pedal stroke will lack power.

These cyclists have their saddles at an ideal height. They will be able to exert power all the way through their pedal stroke.

The importance of biomechanics to cycling does not end here. For example, above a certain speed, most of a cyclist's energy is used battling air resistance. Adjusting your riding position into a racing crouch makes you more aerodynamic, and therefore faster. But below a certain speed, it is better to sit up straight. This makes it easier to get more air into your lungs, while having only a small cost in terms of air resistance.

Like cycling, all sports involving motion are dependent on good biomechanics for top-level performance.

Jan Zelezny

Sport: Javelin

Country: Czechoslovakia, Czech Republic

Born: 16 June 1966

Jan Zelezny is a hero in his home country of the Czech Republic. There and around the world, he is said by many people to be the greatest javelin thrower ever.

Javelin requires great strength and power. Competitors must have an extremely powerful throwing arm, of course. But their technique also requires them to use almost every muscle in their body in throwing the javelin as far as possible.

Zelezny was famous for the speed with which he could whip his throwing arm forwards, launching the javelin with amazing power. He was also remarkable for his ability to produce his greatest performances at big competitions. He dominated javelin throughout the 1990s, winning Olympics gold at the 1992, 1996 and 2000 Games. Although Zelzny was at his best at the Olympics, he also won three World Championships, in 1993, 1995 and 2001.

World records are broken regularly in athletics, and few last more than a year or two. Remarkably, Zelezny's world record of 98.48 m, set in 1996, still stands.

Jan Zelezny about to whip his throwing arm through with blink-and-you-miss-it speed, at his last-ever javelin event.

27

Nutrition

Good nutrition and hydration are important for everyone's heath, not only athletes'. But sports training places particular demands on the body, which makes it especially important that athletes have a good diet.

A balanced diet

For all of us, a balanced diet is crucial for good health. This means eating the right amounts of specific types of food: carbohydrate, protein and fats. Each of these has a different job to do:

- Carbohydrates are the body's main source of energy. The human body needs about 50–60 per cent of its daily calories to come from carbohydrates.

- Fats are a second source of energy, though a less important one for athletes. No more than 20–25 per cent of your daily calories should come from fats.

- Proteins help the body to grow and to repair itself. We need roughly 15–30 per cent of our daily calories to come from proteins.

Bananas are a great, quick source of energy.

A good meal for an athlete mixes plenty of carbohydrates (pasta, vegetables) with some fat (cheese, for example), and a bit of protein (meat or fish).

The protein myth

Some people think that because proteins help muscles grow, eating more proteins will make their muscles grow bigger. This is incorrect. Muscles grow through working hard: for this they need energy, which they get from carbohydrate. Increasing the percentage of protein you eat will mean your body gets a smaller proportion of carbohydrates, and less energy for training. This won't help your strength increase at all!

Weight gain and loss

When training to increase strength, most people will gain weight. Their muscles, and over the medium to long-term their bones, will grow bigger and more dense.

Strength training is generally not a good way to lose weight. If weight loss is required, however, reducing daily calorie intake by no more than 15 per cent will achieve this. A 15 per cent decrease allows athletes to retain hard-earned muscle, but will make it difficult to increase strength or power.

Halil Mutlu on his way to his third Olympic gold medal in a row, this one at the 2004 Athens Games.

PROFESSIONAL PROFILE

Halil Mutlu

Sport: Weightlifting

Country: Bulgaria, Turkey

Born: 14 July 1973

Halil Mutlu is a Bulgarian-born Turkish weightlifter. He is one of only four weightlifters who have won gold medals at three consecutive Olympic Games.

As a young man of 16, Mutlu moved to Turkey from Bulgaria. He was so pleased to arrive that he changed his name from Huben Hubenov to Halil Mutlu. (Mutlu means 'happy' in Turkish.) In 1994, Mutlu won his first international titles, the European and World Championships. It was the start of a long period at the top of the weightlifting world. His successes included:

- winning nine European Championships
- five World Championship victories
- three Olympic gold medals (won in 1996, 2000 and 2004)
- more than 20 world records, set in three different weight divisions

In 2005, Mutlu was banned from competition for two years after testing positive for an illegal anabolic steroid, nandrolone. He claimed never to have knowingly taken drugs, but weightlifting's terrible reputation for drug abuse made people question if this could be true.

Glossary

aerodynamic
able to pass easily through air, without meeting significant air resistance.

air resistance
the slowing-down effect of air as an object passes through it.

anabolic steroids
drugs that can be used to increase muscle mass and strength. The use of steroids in sport is not allowed, because it is risky for athletes' health and gives those who take the drugs an unfair advantage.

anaerobic
without oxygen. Anaerobic energy production happens without the need for oxygen. It produces energy very quickly, but also uses a lot of the muscle's energy stores very quickly.

calorie
measure of the amount of energy contained in food.

central nervous system
brain and spinal cord, which together control and coordinate the body's movements.

clean and jerk
weightlifting technique that allows more weight to be picked up than any other. The lift is done in two stages. First, the lifter pulls the weight up to rest on his or her chest. Second, they thrust it up above their head.

contraction
getting smaller or tightening up.

deadlifting
weightlifting event, in which a heavy object is lifted from the ground to hip height and lowered again in a controlled way.

diabetes
disease of having too much sugar in your blood. This happens because the body stops taking sugar out of blood and turning it into energy stores.

flexibility
ability to move joints through a wide range of movement.

force
physical influence that makes an object move.

genes
code inside your body that decides things such as the colour of your eyes and hair.

joint
part of the body where bones are connected. Many joints can be moved using muscles; others, such as joints in our skulls, cannot.

keirin
track cycling event that began in Japan, but is now raced around the world. The riders at first cycle behind a tiny moped, which slowly begins to travel faster. Shortly before the end of the race, the moped reaches about 50kph and pulls off the track, after which the riders sprint for the finish.

ligament
tough fibres that support a joint and help it to keep its shape.

masters
sports event for older people.

powerlifting
weightlifting event that combines three different kinds of lift, the squat, bench press, and dead lift.

pursuit
cycling race in which two riders start on opposite sides of the track and try to catch one another up. If both fail to do so, the first one to finish a set distance is the winner.

range of movement
amount of movement possible from one extreme to the other.

scull
race with each rower in a boat using two oars, one on each side.

stall
slow down or stop moving forwards.

stimulants
drug that increase the body's activity, mainly by increasing heart rate.

tendon
strong fibre that attaches muscle to bone.

torso
trunk; central part of body, ending at the neck, shoulders and hips.

trunk
see torso.

Further information

BOOKS TO READ

Body: An Amazing Tour of Human Anatomy by Robert Winston (editor) (Dorling Kindersley, 2005)

The Complete Guide To Sports Training by John Shepherd (A&C Black, 2006)
This book has useful workouts for a variety of sports, and a good section on speed training.

The Complete Guide to Strength Training by Anita Bean (A&C Black, 2008)
A former British Bodybuilding Champion gives a wealth of advice about building up muscle strength. The book it strong on weight training, and contains useful weight sessions for a variety of sports.

Goal! Science Projects With Soccer; Wheels! Science Projects With Bicycles, Skateboards and Skates by Madeline Goodstein; and *Slam Dunk! Science Projects With Basketball*, by Robert Gardner and Dennis Shortelle (Enslow Publishers, 2009)

Our Bodies by Steve Parker (Wayland, 2006)
This series provides the essential knowledge about anatomy you need as a sportsperson.

Plyometrics for Explosive Speed and Power by Neal Pire (Ulysses Press, 2006)
Aimed at sportspeople of all abilities and levels, this excellent book contains basic information about plyometrics, plus over 70 exercises. There are specific sets for basketball, cycling, gymnastics, rugby, football, swimming, track and field, and more.

Sports Science by various authors (Franklin Watts, 2009)
A series that takes a look at popular sports, such as football and tennis, and the science behind them.

WEBSITES

www.brianmac.co.uk/
Brian Mac is a senior coach for UK Athletics, the governing body for track and field in the UK. He has 40 years of experience as an endurance athlete, and over 25 years as a coach, and most of his experience is found somewhere on this exhaustive, but easy to navigate, website.

http://www.sport-fitness-advisor.com/speedtraining.html
This section of the sport fitness advisor site has basic information on the requirements of speed training, plus links to a huge variety of articles on improving your sprinting technique, drills for speed and agility, speed endurance and much more.

Index